cooking the Caribbean way

Asopao is a chicken and rice stew that is related to the famous Spanish dish called paella. (Recipe on page 22.)

cooking the
Caribbean way

CHERYL DAVIDSON KAUFMAN

PHOTOGRAPHS BY ROBERT L. AND DIANE WOLFE

easy menu
ethnic
cookbooks

Lerner Publications Company ▪ Minneapolis

Editor: Vicki Revsbech
Drawings by Jeanette Swofford
Map by J. Michael Roy

Photograph on page 10 courtesy of the Jamaica
Tourist Board

The publisher wishes to thank Eunice Revsbech for her
assistance in the preparation of this book.

The page border for this book is a shell pattern.

To the memory of Gaga, who always believed in
everything I did

Library of Congress Cataloging-in-Publication Data

Kaufman, Cheryl Davidson.
  Cooking the Caribbean way.

  (Easy menu ethnic cookbooks)
  Includes index.
  Summary: Presents a history of Caribbean cooking
and recipes for daily menus.
    1. Cookery, Caribbean — Juvenile literature.
2. Caribbean Area — Social life and customs — Juvenile
literature. | 1. Cookery, Caribbean. 2. Caribbean Area —
Social life and customs| I. Title. II. Series.
TX716.A1K38 1988   641.59′ 1821   87-37850
ISBN 0-8225-0920-2 (lib. bdg.)

Manufactured in the United States of America

4 5 6 7 8 9 10 97 96 95 94 93 92

**Apple cider vinegar and spices such as garlic and
ginger give Betty's browned-down chicken a tangy
flavor. (Recipe on page 31.)**

CONTENTS

INTRODUCTION, 7
  The Land, 7
  History, 8
  The Food, 9
  Christmas in Jamaica, 11

WORKING WITH COCONUT, 12

BEFORE YOU BEGIN, 13
  Cooking Utensils, 13
  Cooking Terms, 14
  Special Ingredients, 14

A CARIBBEAN MENU, 16

SOUPS AND STEWS, 18
  Pepperpot Soup, 18
  Callaloo, 19
  Pepperpot Stew, 21
  Asopao, 22

SIDE DISHES, 23
  Cornmeal Coo-coo, 23
  Rice and Peas, 25
  Akkra, 26
  Johnny Cakes, 26

Foo-foo, 27

MAIN DISHES, 28
  Stamp and Go, 28
  Escovitch Fish, 30
  Betty's Browned-down Chicken, 31
  Jamaican Beef Patties, 32
  Curried Lamb, 34
  Caribbean-style Rice, 36
  Jug Jug, 36

DESSERTS, 38
  Coconut Ice, 38
  Sweet Potato Pone, 40
  Duckunoo, 40
  Banana Fritters, 41

BEVERAGES, 42
  Ginger Beer, 42
  Peanut Punch, 43

THE CAREFUL COOK, 44

METRIC CONVERSION CHART, 45

INDEX, 45

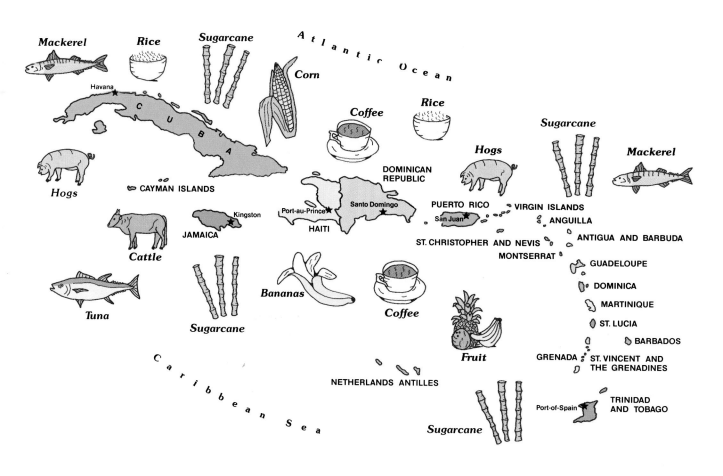

Mackerel

Rice

Sugarcane

Atlantic Ocean

Corn

Coffee

Rice

Havana

C U B A

Hogs

Sugarcane

Mackerel

Hogs

☙ CAYMAN ISLANDS

DOMINICAN
REPUBLIC

Kingston

Port-au-Prince ★   Santo Domingo ★

PUERTO RICO   ⟡ VIRGIN ISLANDS

San Juan ★   ⟡ ANGUILLA

JAMAICA

HAITI

ST. CHRISTOPHER AND NEVIS ⟡   ANTIGUA AND BARBUDA

MONTSERRAT ⟡

Cattle

GUADELOUPE

DOMINICA

Sugarcane

MARTINIQUE

Bananas

Coffee

ST. LUCIA

Tuna

BARBADOS

GRENADA ⟡ ST. VINCENT AND
THE GRENADINES

Fruit

Caribbean Sea

NETHERLANDS ANTILLES

Sugarcane

Port-of-Spain ★ TRINIDAD
AND TOBAGO

INTRODUCTION

If there is one word that can be used to describe life on a Caribbean island, it is variety. In one day, you might see a flying fish, enjoy a very British tea party, and dance to the music of a steel band. The food of the Caribbean is a particularly diverse blend of tastes and textures that differs somewhat from island to island. The cuisine takes advantage of the abundance of fresh foods on the islands, while it also reflects the tastes and traditions of the people who have come to the Caribbean over the years from different parts of the world.

THE LAND

The islands of the Caribbean—about 30 large and several thousand small—stretch from Cuba in the north to Trinidad in the south. Cuba lies just off the coast of Florida, and there are points on the coast of Trinidad that are only 25 miles from South America.

The Caribbean is often described as a kind of paradise. Miles and miles of black and white sand beaches line the clear blue waters of the Caribbean Sea. Forested mountains overlook valleys overflowing with fruit trees, sugarcane, orchids, and ferns. But there is another side to this paradise. Many of the mountains are actually active volcanoes. Bright 80° days can suddenly give way to fierce cloudbursts that wash away everything in their paths.

While the Caribbean islands may appear to be very similar, they are not all the same. Some islands are much larger than the others. In fact, Cuba is nearly as big as the rest of the islands combined. Other islands are so small that they are little more than mounds of coral peeking out of the ocean. The Caribbean's smallest islands are likely to be uninhabited, while some of the other islands are quite crowded. Overall, the Caribbean is home to about 31 million people.

There are also differences in terrain and vegetation from island to island. Some islands are mountainous and others are almost completely flat. It may come as a surprise to learn that not all of the islands are tropical. There are desertlike areas that receive little rain.

HISTORY

Nearly 1000 years ago, the Arawak and the Carib Indians were the only people inhabiting the Caribbean islands. The Arawaks were gentle people who were skillful farmers. The Caribs, on the other hand, were warlike and often raided other islands. The Indians had the islands to themselves until 1492, when Christopher Columbus arrived in the Caribbean.

When Columbus realized the fortune that could be made in sugarcane and tobacco in the Caribbean, he claimed nearly all of the islands for Spain. But it wasn't long before other European countries recognized the riches the Caribbean had to offer.

The first to defy Spain's claim to the islands were the French and English pirates—or buccaneers—that overran the Caribbean during the 1500s and 1600s. Many pirates made Port Royal Harbor in Kingston, Jamaica, their home base. The city was often called "the wickedest port on earth" because of the gold coins, precious jewels, and other stolen property that ended up there. Port Royal was destroyed by an earthquake in 1692 during which much of this bounty sank to the bottom of the sea.

During the 1600s, Spain's power declined and other Europeans began to settle in the Caribbean, including the French, Dutch, Portuguese, and English. The European settlers brought black slaves from Africa to work on their plantations. Meanwhile, the Arawak Indians had become extinct within 100 years of the coming of the Spanish. The Caribs had fought bravely for many years, but as their numbers diminished, they began to intermarry with other nationalities who came to the islands.

Today, many of the islands are proudly independent of the European countries that once ruled them. There are still, however, important ties between certain countries in Europe, such as Great Britain and France, and the Caribbean. Independence has brought a surge of nationalism, an exploration of old Caribbean traditions, and a strong desire to maintain economic and cultural exchanges between the islands.

THE FOOD

Today, the Caribbean is a melting pot of different cultures and traditions. The ancestors of a Caribbean islander may be black, Spanish, British, French, Dutch, Portuguese, East Indian, Chinese, or any combination of nationalities. I was born in Jamaica, so I am most familiar with Jamaican traditions.

One of my early memories as a child is being placed in a bathtub with a huge, juicy mango peeled and ready to eat. I could get as messy as I liked with that dripping, sweet juice and then be cleaned up in the same spot when I was done. Mangoes are just one of the fruits that grow in the Caribbean. In my own backyard, there were lime and banana trees; coconut, avocado, and breadfruit trees; custard-apple, soursop, and ackee trees.

Aside from fruit trees, my family had a garden, several hens, and one very mean rooster. I enjoyed being sent out to pick fresh vegetables such as red peppers or "skellions" (green onions) from the garden to add to whatever was being cooked on the stove at the moment. When one of us was sick or hurt, the garden could immediately supply mint (two kinds) for tea, leaf-of-life for coughs, and sinkle-bible (aloe) for cuts and bruises.

The kitchen was always the hub of activity at my house, and I spent a lot of time there waiting to be put to work or hoping for a taste of something. Sometimes I would shell beans, which we called peas, fresh from the garden or watch my mother "season up" meat for the next day. All good Caribbean cooks season their meat at least a few hours before cooking it, if not a day ahead. The meat is rubbed with salt, black pepper, garlic, fresh hot pepper, and onion, as well as any other spices the cook chooses to use. My mother never measured the spices. Her hands just seemed to know exactly how much to add.

Though there are supermarkets in Jamaica, we bought many of our fruits and vegetables at the open-air market, where everything was guaranteed to be fresh. Rows of vendors, each with a scale, would offer an endless supply of callaloo greens, chocho, garden egg (eggplant), Irish or sweet potatoes, white

A vendor sells fruits and vegetables at a colorful market stall in Jamaica.

or yellow yams, dasheen (taro root), tomatoes, and—when in season—naseberries, otaheite apples, and tamarind. The smells, colors, and textures of the market are overwhelming and must be experienced to be appreciated.

CHRISTMAS IN JAMAICA

Delicious, carefully prepared food is an important part of Jamaican holidays—especially Christmas. In my family, preparations started weeks before Christmas, when we made food to serve to the guests that would visit our home. In Jamaica, guests are traditionally offered fruitcake, slices of cold ham, and sorrel during the Christmas season.

Baking the traditional fruitcakes was a day-long event. We sometimes made as many as 20 of the dense cakes, so every pair of hands was important. I would separate dozens of eggs and sift cup after cup of flour. For hours, the house would be filled with the rich smell of baking cakes, and nothing could beat the first taste from the small sample cake we always made.

As Christmas neared, preparations intensified. We boiled a giant country-cured ham over a fire in our backyard and then decorated it with cloves and basted it with fresh pineapple juice, brown sugar, and mustard before squeezing it into the oven to bake. We also made sorrel. Sorrel is a refreshing, gingery drink made from the waxy sepals of the sorrel plant. We steeped the sepals in hot water, strained and sweetened the liquid, and served it over ice.

There was always plenty to eat on Christmas Day. In the morning, we ate big slices of sweet potato pudding. Christmas dinner was a huge meal. We had turkey, ham, chicken, curried goat, rice and peas, ackee and codfish, and several kinds of salads and vegetables. Dinner always ended with slices of fruitcake or boiled plum pudding and glasses of sorrel served on the verandah, or porch, where the whole family would retire to recover from the meal.

Although I now live in the United States, I still follow Caribbean traditions of cooking and hospitality. I hope you will enjoy sharing these "back home" recipes with your friends as much as I have.

WORKING WITH COCONUT

How to Crack Open a Coconut

1. Puncture the three "eyes" on one end of the coconut by driving a nail or a screwdriver through the center of each one with a hammer.

2. Pour the liquid out of the coconut.

3. Rap the coconut sharply on the side with a hammer to split it in half.

4. Remove the hard outer shell from the coconut meat.

5. The brown skin under the shell can be removed from the coconut meat with a knife or a vegetable peeler.

How to Make Coconut Milk

1. Coconut milk can be made with either fresh or packaged coconut. If using fresh coconut, grate by hand or break coconut meat into pieces and grate in a blender or food processor with 1 to 2 tablespoons hot water.

2. Place 2 cups grated coconut in a large bowl. Add 2 cups hot water and stir.

3. When coconut mixture is cool enough to handle, pick up clumps of coconut from the water and squeeze to express a white milky liquid back into the bowl. Continue to squeeze coconut in bowl for 4 to 5 minutes.

4. Pour coconut milk through a strainer with another large bowl underneath to catch the liquid. Discard coconut. Coconut milk can be used in many recipes, from main dishes to desserts.

BEFORE YOU BEGIN

Cooking any dish, plain or fancy, is easier and more fun if you are familiar with its ingredients. Caribbean cooking makes use of some ingredients that you may not know. You should also be familiar with the special terms that will be used in various recipes in this book. Therefore, *before* you start cooking any of the Caribbean dishes in this book, study the following "dictionary" of special terms very carefully. Then read through the recipe you want to try from beginning to end.

Now you are ready to shop for ingredients and to organize the cookware you will need. Once you have assembled everything, you can begin to cook. It is also important to read *The Careful Cook* on page 44 before you start. Following these rules will make your cooking experience safe, fun, and easy.

COOKING UTENSILS

cheesecloth—A gauzy cotton cloth that can be used as a strainer

colander—A bowl with holes in the bottom and sides. It is used for draining liquid from a solid food.

cooking bags—Plastic bags that can be used to hold food while it is being cooked in boiling water

grater—A utensil with sharp-edge holes, used to grate food into small pieces

rolling pin—A cylindrical tool used for rolling out dough

sieve—A bowl-shaped utensil made of wire mesh used to drain small, fine foods

slotted spoon—A spoon with small openings in the bowl. It is used to pick solid food out of a liquid.

tongs—A utensil shaped either like tweezers or scissors with flat, blunt ends used to grasp food

COOKING TERMS

beat – To stir rapidly in a circular motion

boil – To heat a liquid over high heat until bubbles form and rise rapidly to the surface

brown – To cook food quickly with high heat so that the surface turns an even brown

core – To remove the center part of a fruit or vegetable

grate – To cut into tiny pieces by rubbing the food against a grater

sauté – To fry quickly over high heat in oil or fat, stirring or turning the food to prevent burning

scald – To heat a liquid (such as milk) to a temperature just below its boiling point

seed – To remove seeds from a food

sift – To put an ingredient, such as flour, through a sifter to break up any lumps

simmer – To cook over low heat in liquid kept just below its boiling point. Bubbles may occasionally rise to the surface.

SPECIAL INGREDIENTS

allspice – The berry of a West Indian tree, used whole or ground, whose flavor resembles a combination of cinnamon, nutmeg, and cloves

black-eyed peas – Small, tan peas with a large black spot from which they get their name

cassareep – The juice from the cassava root. To make cassareep, grate a peeled cassava root into a sieve. With the back of a spoon, press the juice from the cassava root through the sieve into a small saucepan. Cook the liquid over medium heat for one or two minutes or until it thickens.

chilies – Small hot red or green peppers

cinnamon – A spice made from the bark of a tree in the laurel family, which is available ground and in sticks

cloves – Dried buds from a small evergreen tree that can be used whole or ground to flavor food

coconut cream – A thick, sweet coconut mixture available in cans at most grocery stores

coconut milk—A liquid made of grated coconut and milk that is often used in Caribbean cooking. Instructions for how to make coconut milk are on page 12.

cornmeal—Coarsely ground dried corn

cream of tartar—A white, powdery substance often used in baking

curry powder—A mixture of six or more spices that gives food a spicy taste

garlic—An herb whose distinctive flavor is used in many dishes. Each bulb can be broken up into several sections called cloves. Most recipes use only one or two cloves. Before you chop up a clove of garlic, you will have to remove the papery covering that surrounds it.

ginger—A spice made from dried, ground ginger root

ginger root—A knobby, light brown root used to flavor foods

kale—A vegetable related to the cabbage with loose, curly leaves

lard—Soft animal fat used in cooking

monosodium glutamate—A white granular substance used to enhance the flavor of food

nutmeg—A fragrant spice, either whole or ground, that is often used in desserts

okra—The small, green pods of the okra plant, which can be eaten as a vegetable

oregano—The dried leaves, whole or ground, of a rich and fragrant herb, which are used as a seasoning

paprika—Dried ground sweet red peppers used for its flavor and its red color

peppercorns—The berries of an East Indian plant. Peppercorns are used both whole and ground (pepper) to flavor food.

plantain—A starchy fruit that looks like a banana and must be cooked before it is eaten

suet—Hard animal fat that can be used in cooking. It is available from your butcher.

thyme—A fragrant herb used fresh or dried to season food

yeast—An ingredient used in cooking to make bread rise and cause liquid to ferment

A CARIBBEAN MENU

Below are suggested menus for a variety of Caribbean meals. Recipes for the starred items can be found in this book.

MENU	*ISLAND*
Breakfast	
*Johnny Cakes	All Islands
*Stamp and Go	Jamaica
Fresh Fruit	
Milk or Mint Tea	
Lunch	
I	
*Pepperpot Soup or	Jamaica
*Callaloo	All Islands
*Foo-foo	All Islands
Homemade Bread	
Fresh Fruit	
II	
*Jamaican Beef Patties	Jamaica
*Peanut Punch	Trinidad and Tobago
Beach Picnic	
*Escovitch Fish or	Jamaica
*Asopao	Puerto Rico
*Rice and Peas	Trinidad and Tobago/Jamaica
*Akkra	Jamaica
*Banana Fritters	All Islands

MENU	ISLAND
Fresh Fruit	
Coconut Water	
Fruit Juice	
Formal Dinner	
*Betty's Browned-down Chicken	Trinidad and Tobago
Lettuce and Tomato Salad	
*Rice and Peas	Trinidad and Tobago/Jamaica
*Cornmeal Coo-coo	Barbados
*Coconut Ice	Barbados
Supper	
I	
*Curried Lamb	Jamaica
*Caribbean-style Rice	All Islands
Fresh Fruit Salad	
*Stamp and Go or	Jamaica
*Banana Fritters	All Islands
*Sweet Potato Pone or	Barbados
*Duckunoo	Jamaica
*Ginger Beer	Trinidad and Tobago
II	
*Jug Jug or	Barbados
*Pepperpot Stew	All Islands
Fried Plantains	
*Ginger Beer	Trinidad and Tobago

SOUPS AND STEWS

Stews and soups are favorite informal meals in the Caribbean. They can contain one or several kinds of meat, poultry, or seafood and just about any other ingredient that is available, from olives to okra. Stews are thicker than soups and are sometimes served over rice, while soups are often served with foo-foo.

Pepperpot Soup
Jamaica

This flavorful soup is usually served on Saturday, a popular soup-eating day in Jamaican homes.

4 cups water
½ pound beef stew meat, cut into bite-sized pieces
1 ¼-pound smoked ham hock
1 pound fresh spinach with stems removed, finely chopped
¼ pound kale, finely chopped
5 ounces frozen okra, thawed
2 medium potatoes, peeled and diced

1 small onion, peeled and chopped
2 green onions, chopped
1 small chili, seeded and chopped
1 clove garlic, peeled and crushed
1 sprig fresh thyme or a pinch dried thyme
¾ cup coconut milk (see page 12)

1. In a large kettle, bring 4 cups water to a boil over high heat. Add beef, ham hock, spinach, kale, okra, and potatoes. Reduce heat to low, cover, and simmer for about 1 hour or until meat is tender.
2. Pour soup through a sieve with another large kettle underneath to catch liquid.
3. Set meat aside. With the back of a spoon, rub vegetables through sieve into liquid.
4. Add onions, green onions, chili, garlic, and thyme. Simmer until soup starts to thicken. Add coconut milk and stir well.
5. Remove meat from ham hock, cut into bite-sized pieces, and add to soup. Add beef and stir well.
6. Cook 10 minutes more and serve hot.

Serves 6

Callaloo
All Islands

*This soup is traditionally made with calla-
loo greens, which were introduced to the
Caribbean by the Africans. When I was
growing up, I didn't like plain boiled callaloo greens, but I loved this combination of
callaloo, crabmeat, coconut milk, and
spices.*

4 tablespoons butter or margarine
1 small onion, chopped
1 clove garlic, peeled and chopped
**¾ pound fresh spinach with stems
     removed, finely chopped**
3 cups chicken broth
½ cup coconut milk (see page 12)
1 medium potato, peeled and chopped
1 teaspoon salt
1½ teaspoons black pepper
**½ pound cooked crabmeat (fresh,
     canned, or frozen and thawed)**
paprika

1. In a large kettle, melt butter over
medium-high heat. Add onions and garlic
and sauté for about 5 minutes or until onion
is transparent. Add spinach and cook for
5 minutes, stirring to coat with butter.
Remove spinach from kettle and set aside.
2. Add chicken broth, coconut milk,
potato, salt, and black pepper to kettle
and stir well. Bring to a boil over high heat.
3. Reduce heat to low and cover, leaving
cover slightly ajar. Simmer for 15 minutes
or until potato can be easily pierced with
a fork.
4. Add spinach and simmer, uncovered,
for 10 minutes or until spinach is tender.
5. Add crabmeat and stir well. Cook for
another 5 minutes or until heated through.
Sprinkle with paprika and serve hot.

Serves 4 to 6

Caribbean soups and stews like pepperpot soup *(left)*, pepperpot stew *(center)*, and callaloo *(right)* are hearty enough to be served as a meal.

Pepperpot Stew
All Islands

Cassareep, which is the juice from the cassava root, gives pepperpot stew a distinctive bittersweet flavor.

1 chili
3 whole cloves
1 2-inch stick cinnamon
2 to 3 pounds chicken (5 to 6 pieces)
1 ¼-pound ham hock
5 cups water
1 teaspoon salt
1 pound boneless pork, cut into bite-sized pieces
1 small onion, peeled and chopped
¼ teaspoon dried thyme
1 tablespoon molasses
¼ cup cassareep (optional, see page 14)
2 teaspoons white vinegar

1. Cut out a 5- by 5-inch piece of cheesecloth. Place whole chili, cloves, and cinnamon stick in center of cloth. Gather cloth around ingredients to form a bag and tie closed with a piece of string.
2. In a large kettle, combine chicken, ham hock, 5 cups water, and salt. Bring to a boil over high heat. Reduce heat to low, cover, and simmer for 1 hour.
3. Skim foam off top of liquid with a spoon and discard. Add pork, onions, thyme, molasses, and cassareep and stir well. Add cheesecloth bag.
4. Bring to a boil over high heat. Reduce heat to low, cover, and simmer for about 45 minutes or until pork is tender.
5. With a fork or tongs, remove cheesecloth bag and discard. Remove ham hock and set aside. Stir in vinegar.
6. When ham hock is cool, remove meat, cut into bite-sized pieces, and add to stew. Stir well and heat for 4 or 5 minutes more. Serve with Caribbean-style rice (see page 36).

Serves 6

Asopao
Puerto Rico

The word asopao *means "soupy" in Spanish.*

- **1 clove garlic, peeled and chopped**
- **2 pounds chicken (4 to 5 pieces)**
- **¼ cup all-purpose flour**
- **½ teaspoon salt**
- **1 teaspoon black pepper**
- **½ teaspoon dried oregano**
- **2 tablespoons lard or shortening**
- **½ medium green pepper, cored and chopped**
- **1 small onion, peeled and chopped**
- **1 ounce ham, diced (about ¼ cup)**
- **2 medium tomatoes, chopped**
- **3 cups chicken broth**
- **1 cup uncooked long-grain white rice**
- **1 10-ounce package frozen green peas, thawed**
- **¼ cup stuffed green olives**
- **¼ cup grated Parmesan cheese**

1. In a small bowl, mash garlic with the back of a spoon. Rub garlic into chicken.
2. In a wide, shallow bowl combine flour, salt, black pepper, and oregano. Roll chicken pieces in flour mixture.
3. In a large kettle, melt lard over medium-high heat. Add chicken and cook for 8 to 10 minutes or until brown. Remove from kettle and set aside.
4. Add green pepper and onions to kettle and sauté until onions are transparent.
5. Stir in ham and tomatoes. Cook over medium heat for 10 minutes.
6. Return chicken to kettle and stir well. Reduce heat to low, cover, and cook for 30 minutes or until chicken is tender.
7. Remove chicken from tomato mixture. When cool, remove meat from bones and cut into bite-sized pieces.
8. Add chicken broth and rice to tomato mixture and stir well. Bring to a boil over high heat, Reduce heat to low and cover, placing a paper towel between the kettle and the lid. Simmer for 20 minutes.
9. Add peas, olives, Parmesan cheese, and chicken and stir well. Cover and cook for 5 more minutes.

Serves 4 to 6

SIDE DISHES

These mild-flavored side dishes can be paired with spicier main dishes to round out a Caribbean meal. Akkra can also be eaten as an appetizer, and rice and peas is hearty enough to serve alone for lunch or for a light supper.

Cornmeal Coo-coo
Barbados

This recipe calls for okra, a small, green vegetable from West Africa.

3 tablespoons butter or margarine
1 medium onion, peeled and chopped
2 cups water
1 10-ounce package frozen okra, thawed
1 cup yellow cornmeal

1. In a small frying pan, melt 1 tablespoon butter over medium heat. Add onions and sauté until transparent. Remove from heat and set aside.
2. In a large saucepan, bring 2 cups of water to a boil over high heat. Add okra and reduce heat to low.
3. Slowly pour cornmeal into water while stirring constantly. Cook for 7 or 8 minutes, stirring constantly, until mixture begins to thicken.
4. Add remaining butter and onions and stir. Pour into a shallow serving dish and smooth the top with a knife. Serve immediately.

Serves 6

These side dishes make a Caribbean meal complete. Pictured are *(clockwise starting top right)* cornmeal coo-coo, johnny cakes, akkra, foo-foo, and rice and peas.

Rice and Peas

Trinidad and Tobago, Jamaica

When I was growing up, no Sunday dinner at my house was complete without rice and peas, a dish that is just as tasty eaten by itself as it is served with meat and gravy. In the Caribbean, beans are called peas.

1 cup dried red kidney beans
4 cups coconut milk (see page 12)
1 clove garlic, peeled and chopped, or
    1 teaspoon garlic powder
2 green onions
3 sprigs fresh thyme or ¼ teaspoon
    dried thyme
1 teaspoon salt
½ teaspoon black pepper
3 cups water
3 cups uncooked long-grain white rice

1. Place beans in a colander and rinse well with cold water.
2. In a large saucepan, combine beans with enough water to cover them, then add coconut milk and garlic. Bring to a boil over high heat. Reduce heat to low and cover, leaving cover slightly ajar. Simmer for about 1½ hours or until beans are tender. Do not overcook.
3. Add green onions, thyme, salt, black pepper, 3 cups water, and rice. Bring to a boil over high heat. Reduce heat to low and cover tightly, placing a paper towel between saucepan and lid. Simmer for 20 minutes.
4. Remove cover and stir gently with a fork. Rice grains should be separate and fluffy and water should be absorbed. If not done, cover and continue to cook, checking every 5 minutes until done.

Serves 6 to 8

Akkra
Jamaica

Akkra is sometimes made with salt fish instead of ground peas.

2　cups dried black-eyed peas
6　chilies
⅓　cup water
　　vegetable oil for frying

1. Place peas in a large saucepan and cover with water. Let soak overnight.
2. Rub peas together between your palms to remove skins. Skins will float to top of water and can be skimmed off. Let peas soak for another 2 hours after skins are removed.
3. Place peas in a blender, 1 cup at a time, and blend about 20 seconds until smooth. Remove ground peas from blender, place in a a large bowl, and repeat with remaining peas.
4. Cut chilies in half and remove stems and seeds. Place in blender and blend about 20 seconds.
5. Add ground chilies to peas and stir. If mixture is dry, stir in water, little by little, until pasty. Beat with a spoon until light and fluffy.
6. Pour 1 inch of oil into a large frying pan and heat for 4 or 5 minutes over medium-high heat. Carefully drop rounded table-spoons of pea mixture into oil and fry 2 to 3 minutes per side or until golden brown. Remove from oil with slotted spoon and drain on paper towels.

Serves 6

Johnny Cakes
All Islands

These fried biscuits are called bakes in Trinidad and Tobago and johnny cakes on the other islands. They are delicious with stamp and go or fried sprats.

2　cups all-purpose flour
½　teaspoon salt
1　teaspoon baking powder
1　tablespoon plus 2 teaspoons butter or
　　margarine, softened
¼　cup cold water
　　vegetable oil for frying

1. Sift flour, salt, and baking powder together into a large bowl.
2. With clean hands, rub butter into flour mixture until mixture is grainy. Stir in water, little by little, until dough can be formed into a ball but is not sticky.
3. Place dough on a clean, flat surface that has been dusted with flour. Dust a rolling pin with flour and roll out dough to about ¼-inch thickness. Dip the rim of a glass in flour and cut dough into circles. Repeat with remaining dough until all dough has been used up.
4. Pour ¼ inch oil into medium frying pan and heat over medium-high heat for 4 or 5 minutes.
5. Fry biscuits a few at a time for 3 or 4 minutes per side or until golden brown. Remove with slotted spoon and drain on paper towels.

Makes 10 to 12 biscuits

Foo-foo
All Islands

Foo-foo is a tasty addition to home-made soups.

5 medium unpeeled green plantains
½ teaspoon salt
¼ teaspoon black pepper

1. Place unpeeled plantains in a large kettle and cover with water. Bring to a boil over high heat. Boil 15 or 20 minutes or until plantains can be pierced with a fork.
2. Remove plantains from water with tongs. When cool enough to handle, remove peel.
3. In a medium bowl, mash plantains well with a fork. Add salt and black pepper and beat with a spoon until mixture forms a thick paste.
4. Roll foo-foo into 1½-inch balls. Serve with soup.

Serves 6

MAIN DISHES

Caribbean cuisine features a wide variety of main dishes. While most of these dishes contain some sort of meat, poultry, or seafood, they are usually not expensive to prepare. Caribbean cooks know how to take inexpensive cuts of meat and simple ingredients and turn them into something special. The secret is skillful seasoning and cooking methods that bring out the flavor in food.

Stamp and Go
Jamaica

In my family, these fritters were a special Sunday morning breakfast treat.

½ **pound salt codfish**
1 **medium onion, peeled and chopped**
2 **green onions, chopped**
1 **small clove garlic, chopped, or ¼ teaspoon garlic powder**
4 **cherry tomatoes, chopped**
1 **chili, seeded and chopped**
4 **cups all-purpose flour**
2 **teaspoons baking powder**
½ **cup water**
2 **tablespoons butter or margarine, melted**
½ **teaspoon paprika vegetable oil for frying**

1. Place codfish in a medium bowl and cover with water. Soak for about 30 minutes.
2. Drain in a colander. Remove bones if necessary. Place fish in a medium bowl and break apart with a fork into flakes.
3. Add onions, green onions, garlic, tomatoes, and chili and stir.
4. Stir in flour, baking powder, ½ cup water, butter, and paprika.
5. Pour 1 inch oil into a large frying pan and heat over medium-high heat for 4 or 5 minutes. Carefully drop tablespoons of batter into oil. Fry until golden brown and crisp on both sides.
6. Remove from oil with slotted spoon and drain on paper towels. Keep warm in a 200° oven until ready to serve. Serve hot.

Serves 6

Escovitch fish *(left)* and stamp and go *(right)* are two recipes that take advantage of the abundance of seafood in the Caribbean.

Escovitch Fish
Jamaica

This recipe can be made with any firm whitefish, such as halibut. The name escovitch *comes from the Spanish word* escobeche, *which means "pickled."*

3 pounds firm whitefish, cut into 4 slices, ½ inch thick
2 large lemons or 6 tablespoons lemon juice
2 cups water
4 teaspoons salt
4 teaspoons black pepper
½ cup vegetable oil for frying
2 cups white or malt vinegar
2 large onions, peeled and sliced
1 teaspoon whole black peppercorns
1 chili, seeded and cut in strips
1 teaspoon whole allspice

1. Place fish in a medium bowl. Squeeze lemons over fish and add 2 cups water. Cover lightly with plastic wrap and refrigerate for 1 hour. Drain fish in a colander and dry thoroughly with paper towels.

2. In a wide, shallow bowl, combine salt and black pepper. Coat fish on both sides with salt and black pepper.

3. In a large frying pan, heat oil over medium-high heat for 4 or 5 minutes. Carefully place fish in oil with tongs and fry 5 minutes per side or until fish is crisp and flaky. Do not overcook or fish will fall apart. Remove from oil and place in a deep glass dish.

4. Add vinegar, onions, peppercorns, chili, and allspice to oil in frying pan and stir well. Bring to a boil over high heat. Reduce heat to low, cover, and simmer 10 to 15 minutes or until onions are tender. Remove from heat.

5. Pour vinegar mixture over fish, cover, and refrigerate for at least 1 hour. Serve hot or cold.

Serves 4 to 6

Betty's Browned-down Chicken
Trinidad and Tobago

Every Caribbean cook has a recipe for chicken with an original twist in seasoning. "Browning down" gives meat a golden brown color and makes a tasty gravy that can be poured over rice and peas.

3 pounds chicken (about 6 pieces)
2 cloves garlic, peeled and crushed
1 medium onion, peeled and sliced
1 chili, seeded and chopped
1 teaspoon salt
½ teaspoon black pepper
1 teaspoon dried thyme
  dash ground ginger
2 tablespoons apple cider vinegar
1 tablespoon sugar
½ cup vegetable oil

1. Wash chicken and rub with garlic. Place in a large bowl and add onions, chili, salt, black pepper, thyme, and ginger. Pour vinegar over chicken, cover tightly, and refrigerate overnight.
2. In a large frying pan, combine sugar and oil. Cook over medium heat, stirring constantly, for 4 or 5 minutes or until sugar has dissolved.
3. Scrape onions off chicken. Do not discard onions or vinegar mixture. Brown chicken, a few pieces at a time, turning to brown all sides evenly.
4. Return browned chicken to pan, add onions and vinegar mixture and enough water to almost cover chicken.
5. Cover and cook over medium heat for 30 minutes or until chicken is tender. Serve meat juices as a gravy.

Serves 4 to 6

Jamaican Beef Patties
Jamaica

Patties are a Jamaican version of "fast food." This inexpensive treat is sold at patty shops all over the island. While beef patties are the most popular, they can also be filled with chicken, lobster, or shrimp.

1 green onion, finely chopped
2 small chilies, seeded and diced
1 pound ground beef
1 to 2 teaspoons salt
1 tablespoon black pepper
½ teaspoon dried thyme
¼ loaf French bread
½ teaspoon paprika
¼ teaspoon monosodium glutamate

1. Place green onions and chilies in a small bowl and grind together with the back of a spoon.
2. In a medium bowl, combine ground beef, salt, black pepper, ¼ teaspoon thyme, and onion mixture and mix well with hands.
3. In a large frying pan, break up meat mixture with a fork and cook over medium-low heat until meat has lost its red color but is not brown. Remove pan from heat and drain off fat.
4. Place bread in a medium saucepan and cover with cold water. Let soak for 5 minutes, then squeeze out bread, saving water.
5. Grind bread in a meat grinder or place in a medium bowl and grind with the back of a spoon.
6. Return bread to soaking water. Add remaining thyme and stir. Cook over medium heat until no liquid remains.
7. Add bread and paprika to meat and mix well. Cook meat mixture over low heat for 20 minutes. Stir in monosodium glutamate, remove from heat, and set aside to cool.

Pastry for Beef Patties:

¾ pound suet
½ teaspoon salt
½ teaspoon curry powder
2¼ cups all-purpose flour
¼ cup ice water

1. Trim fatty membrane from suet. Grate suet through large holes of a grater.
2. In a medium bowl, combine salt, curry powder, and 2 cups flour. Rub suet into flour mixture with hands. Add ice water a little at a time, kneading after each addition, until dough is smooth and not sticky.
3. Form dough into a ball and pat with rolling pin, turning once or twice to make sure it holds together. If it cracks or falls apart, knead in more water. Wrap in foil and place in freezer for at least 1 hour.
4. Preheat oven to 425°.
5. Put ¼ cup flour in a shallow dish. Form a 2-inch piece of dough into a ball and roll in flour. With a rolling pin, roll dough into a 6-inch circle about ⅛ inch thick.
6. Place a heaping tablespoon of meat mixture in center of circle. Fold dough over meat to form a half circle and press outside edge with a fork to seal. Repeat with remaining dough and meat mixture.
7. Place patties on ungreased baking sheet and bake for 35 minutes or until golden brown.

Makes 15 to 16 patties

Jamaican beef patties are pockets of flaky pastry filled with spiced beef.

Curried Lamb

Jamaica

In the Caribbean, this dish is usually made with goat meat instead of lamb. Depending on the cook's taste, curried lamb can be spicy, mild, or anywhere in between.

1¼ **pound lamb shoulder, cubed**
1 **teaspoon salt**
1 **teaspoon black pepper**
2 **cloves garlic, peeled and chopped, or**
    2 tablespoons garlic powder
2 **tablespoons curry powder**
1 **chili, seeded and diced**
1 **medium onion, peeled and diced**
2 **green onions, chopped**
2 **tablespoons vegetable oil**
2 **cups hot water**
2 **medium potatoes, peeled and diced**

1. Place meat in a large bowl and rub with salt, black pepper, garlic, curry powder, chili, onions, and green onions. Cover with plastic wrap and refrigerate for 1 or 2 hours or overnight.
2. In a large frying pan, heat oil over medium heat for 1 minute. Scrape onions off meat and set aside. Brown meat in oil.
3. Add 2 cups hot water and any seasonings left in bowl to meat and stir.
4. Cover pan tightly and cook over medium heat for 45 minutes to 1 hour or until meat is tender.
5. Add potatoes and onions and stir well. Cover and cook about 20 minutes or until potatoes are very soft and gravy has thickened.
6. Serve hot with Caribbean-style rice (see page 36).

Serves 4

Caribbean-style rice helps cool the heat of spicy curried lamb.

Caribbean-style Rice
All Islands

Caribbean islanders like their rice to be fluffy and tender with all of the grains separate. The secret of good rice is to cook it a full 20 minutes without peeking under the lid and letting the steam escape.

4 cups water
1 teaspoon salt
1 tablespoon butter or margarine
2 cups uncooked long-grain rice

1. In a large saucepan, combine 4 cups water, salt, and butter and bring to a boil over high heat.
2. Add rice and stir well with a fork.
3. Reduce heat to low and cover tightly, placing a paper towel between saucepan and lid. Cook for about 20 minutes or until all liquid has been absorbed. *Do not open lid before 20 minutes are up.*
4. Fluff rice with a fork, pour into a serving dish, and serve immediately.

Serves 4 to 6

Jug Jug
Barbados

This dish uses cornmeal, an inexpensive staple that shows up in soups, stews, and desserts all over the Caribbean.

2 cups dried black-eyed peas
½ pound uncooked corned beef
½ pound salt pork
1 medium onion, peeled and cut in half
9 cups water
½ teaspoon dried thyme
½ cup yellow cornmeal
1 teaspoon salt
½ teaspoon black pepper

1. Place peas in a medium bowl and cover with cold water. Let soak overnight.
2. Place corned beef in a medium saucepan and cover with water. Bring to a boil over high heat. Reduce heat to low, cover, and simmer for 3 hours or until beef is tender. Drain beef in a colander and set aside.
3. Drain peas in a colander. In a large

kettle, combine peas, pork, onion, and 9 cups water and bring to a boil over high heat. Reduce heat to low, cover, and simmer for 1½ hours or until peas are tender.

4. Pour pea mixture through a sieve with another large pan underneath to catch the liquid. Return 3 cups of the cooking liquid to the kettle.

5. Finely chop beef, peas, pork, and onion and add to cooking liquid. Add thyme and stir well.

6. Bring mixture to a boil over high heat. Slowly pour cornmeal into water while stirring constantly. Boil, stirring constantly, for 10 minutes or until mixture starts to thicken. Add salt and black pepper and stir well.

7. Reduce heat to low, cover, and simmer for about 20 minutes. Serve hot.

Serves 6

Jug jug is often served at Christmastime on the island of Barbados.

DESSERTS

In the Caribbean, dessert is more likely to be a piece of fresh fruit than a rich chocolate concoction. The islands offer a huge variety of fruit, from pineapples and bananas to the more exotic mangoes, papayas, and custard apples. Desserts made with fruit, including different kinds of pudding, sherbet, and ice cream, are also very popular.

Coconut Ice
Barbados

This sweet and icy coconut treat is a perfect dessert for a hot Caribbean night.

2 cups whole milk
3 cups shredded coconut, fresh or
**   packaged**
1 cup sugar
**   pinch cream of tartar**
1 egg yolk, beaten
**   a few drops almond extract**

1. In a small saucepan, scald milk. Place 2 cups coconut in a sieve. Pour hot milk over coconut while holding sieve over large bowl to catch liquid. Use the back of a spoon to squeeze all of the milk out of the coconut.
2. In a large saucepan, combine coconut milk, sugar, and cream of tartar. Cook over low heat, stirring constantly, until sugar has dissolved.
3. Remove pan from heat and add beaten egg yolk. Beat well with a spoon. Stir in remaining coconut and add 2 or 3 drops almond extract. Taste and add more almond extract if desired.
4. Pour into 2 pie pans. Cover with plastic wrap and place in freezer.
5. Remove coconut ice from freezer after 4 hours and break apart with a fork. Serve immediately.

Serves 4 to 6

Ingredients such as coconut and bananas give these desserts the taste of the islands. Pictured are *(clockwise starting top right)* duckunoo, sweet potato pone, banana fritters, and coconut ice.

Sweet Potato Pone
Barbados

*Sweet potato pone was a Christmas
morning tradition at my house. It was
always a welcome treat after a sunrise
Christmas church service.*

**1 pound raw sweet potatoes, peeled
     and grated (about 1⅔ cups packed)
1 cup whole milk
1 cup coconut cream
1¼ to 1½ cups dark brown sugar
1 teaspoon ginger
1 teaspoon cinnamon
½ teaspoon allspice
1 teaspoon vanilla extract
2 tablespoons melted butter
     or margarine
1 cup hot water
1 cup raisins
2 cups shredded coconut, fresh or
     packaged**

1. Preheat oven to 375°.
2. In a large bowl, combine sweet potatoes,
milk, coconut cream, 1¼ cups brown
sugar, spices, and vanilla extract.
3. Add melted butter, 1 cup hot water,
raisins, and coconut and stir well.
4. Taste mixture for sweetness and add
more brown sugar if desired.
5. Pour into greased 3-quart casserole
dish. Bake for about 1 hour or until mixture is firm in the middle.

Serves 6

Duckunoo
Jamaica

*Duckunoo is sometimes called tie-a-leaf
because in the traditional recipe, the dough
is cooked in banana leaves.*

**3½ cups yellow cornmeal
1½ cups dark brown sugar
 1 teaspoon cinnamon
½ teaspoon allspice
¼ teaspoon salt
1½ cups coconut milk (see page 12)
 2 teaspoons molasses
 1 teaspoon vanilla extract
⅓ cup raisins**

1. In a large bowl, combine cornmeal, brown sugar, cinnamon, allspice, and salt.
2. In a medium bowl, combine coconut milk, molasses, vanilla extract, and raisins.
3. Add coconut-milk mixture to dry ingredients and stir well. Mixture should have the consistency of thick cookie dough. Stir in a few drops of water to thin if necessary.
4. Drop about 2 tablespoons of dough into cooking bag, twist bag closed, and secure with a rubber band or piece of string. Repeat with remaining dough.
5. Fill a large kettle half full of water and bring to a boil over high heat. Carefully drop cooking bags into boiling water and reduce heat to medium-high. Cover, leaving cover slightly ajar to let steam escape. Boil gently for 1½ hours or until mixture is firm.
6. With a slotted spoon, remove bags from water. Dry off bags and unwrap duckunoo. Serve warm or cold.

Makes 12 to 14 bags

Banana Fritters
All Islands

2 large ripe bananas, mashed
3 tablespoons plus 1 teaspoon all-purpose flour
½ teaspoon baking powder
4 tablespoons sugar
dash cinnamon
1 egg, beaten
vegetable oil for frying

1. In a medium bowl, combine bananas, flour, baking powder, 2 tablespoons sugar, cinnamon, and egg and stir well.
2. Pour ½ inch of oil into a large frying pan. Heat oil over medium-high heat for about 4 or 5 minutes.
3. Carefully drop tablespoons of dough into oil and fry for 2 or 3 minutes per side or until golden brown.
4. With a slotted spoon, remove fritters from oil and drain on paper towels. Sprinkle with remaining sugar.

Makes 12 fritters

BEVERAGES

Although a Caribbean islander may start the day with a hot cup of coffee or tea, most Caribbean beverages are served cold. Fruit drinks are very popular and can be made with the juice of just about any of the huge variety of fruits that grow on the islands.

Ginger Beer
Trinidad and Tobago

The sharp taste of ginger gives this drink a refreshingly different flavor.

¾ **cup (¼ pound) grated ginger root**
2 **tablespoons lime juice**
½ **teaspoon cream of tartar**
12 **cups (3 quarts) plus ¼ cup water**
2 **¼-ounce packages active dry yeast**
2 **cups sugar**

1. In a large bowl, combine grated ginger root, lime juice, and cream of tartar and stir well.
2. In a large kettle, bring 12 cups water to a boil over high heat. Carefully pour hot water over ginger mixture and set aside to cool.
3. In a small bowl, combine yeast, ¼ cup water, and ½ cup sugar. Stir to make a smooth paste.
4. When ginger mixture is lukewarm, add yeast mixture and stir well.
5. Cover bowl loosely with plastic wrap and let stand for 3 days.
6. Pour ginger mixture through a sieve with another large bowl underneath to catch the liquid.
7. Add remaining sugar to ginger beer and stir well. Serve chilled over ice.

Makes 3 quarts

Peanut Punch
Trinidad and Tobago

*This thick, rich drink is easy to make
and very filling.*

½ to ⅔ cup smooth peanut butter
3 cups cold whole milk
4 tablespoons sugar
     dash cinnamon
     dash nutmeg

1. Place all ingredients in a blender and
blend on high speed for about 30 seconds
or until thick and frothy.
2. Pour into glasses and serve immediately.
Serves 4

Peanut punch *(left)* **and ginger beer** *(right)* **are perfect accompaniments to a day at the beach.**

THE CAREFUL COOK

Whenever you cook, there are certain safety rules you must always keep in mind.

1. Always wash your hands before handling food.
2. Thoroughly wash all raw vegetables and fruits to remove dirt and chemicals.
3. Use a cutting board when cutting up vegetables and fruits. Don't cut them up in your hand! And be sure to cut in a direction *away* from you and your fingers.
4. Long hair or loose clothing can catch fire if brought near the burners of a stove. If you have long hair, tie it back before cooking.
5. Turn all pot handles toward the back of the stove so that you will not catch your sleeves or jewelry on them. This is especially important when younger brothers and sisters are around. They could easily knock off a pot and get burned.
6. Always use a pot holder to steady hot pots or to take pans out of the oven. Don't use a wet cloth on a hot pan because the steam it produces could burn you.

7. Lift the lid of a steaming pot with the opening away from you so that you will not get burned.
8. If you get burned, hold the burn under cold running water. Do not put grease or butter on it. Cold water helps to take the heat out, but grease or butter will only keep it in.
9. If grease or cooking oil catches fire, throw baking soda or salt at the bottom of the flame to put it out. (Water will *not* put out a grease fire.) Call for help, and try to turn all the stove burners to "off."

HANDLING CHILIES

Fresh chilies have to be handled with care because they contain oils that can burn your eyes or mouth. After working with chilies, be sure not to touch your face until you have washed your hands thoroughly with soap and water. To be extra cautious, wear rubber gloves while fixing chilies. The way you cut the peppers will affect their "hotness." If you take out the seeds, the flavor will be sharp but not fiery. If you leave the seeds in, beware!

METRIC CONVERSION CHART

WHEN YOU KNOW		MULTIPLY BY	TO FIND	
MASS (weight)				
ounces	(oz)	28.0	grams	(g)
pounds	(lb)	0.45	kilograms	(kg)
VOLUME				
teaspoons	(tsp)	5.0	milliliters	(ml)
tablespoons	(Tbsp)	15.0	milliliters	
fluid ounces	(oz)	30.0	milliliters	
cup	(c)	0.24	liters	(l)
pint	(pt)	0.47	liters	
quart	(qt)	0.95	liters	
gallon	(gal)	3.8	liters	
TEMPERATURE				
Fahrenheit	(°F)	5/9 (after	Celsius	(°C)
temperature		subtracting 32)	temperature	

COMMON MEASURES AND THEIR EQUIVALENTS

3 teaspoons = 1 tablespoon
8 tablespoons = ½ cup
2 cups = 1 pint
2 pints = 1 quart
4 quarts = 1 gallon
16 ounces = 1 pound

INDEX

(recipes indicated by **bold face** *type)*

A
akkra, 24, **26**
allspice, 14
asopao, 2, **22**

B
banana fritters, 39, **41**
Barbados
    coconut ice, **38,** 39
    cornmeal coo-coo, **23,** 24
    jug jug, **36-37**
    sweet potato pone, 39, **40**
beat, 14
beef
    jug jug, **36-37**
    patties, Jamaican, **32-33**
before you begin, 13
Betty's browned-down chicken, 4, **31**
beverages, 42
    ginger beer, **42,** 43
    peanut punch, **43**
black-eyed peas, 14
    akkra, 24, **26**
boil, 14
brown, 14

C
callaloo, **19,** 20
careful cook, the, 44
Caribbean
    Christmas in, 11
    food of, 9-11
    history of, 8

land of, 7
map of, 6
menu, 16-17
-style rice, 35, **36**
cassareep, 14
cheesecloth, 13
chicken
asopao, 2, **22**
Betty's browned-down, 4, **31**
chilies, 14
cinnamon, 14
cloves, 14
coconut
cream, 14
how to crack open, 12
ice, **38**, 39
coconut milk, 15
how to make, 12
colander, 13
cooking
bags, 13
terms, 14
utensils, 13
core, 14
cornmeal, 15
coo-coo, **23**, 24
cream of tartar, 15
curried lamb, **34**, 35
curry powder, 15

D
desserts, 38
banana fritters, 39, **41**
coconut ice, **38**, 39
duckunoo, 39, **40-41**
sweet potato pone, 39, **40**
duckunoo, 39, **40-41**

E
escovitch fish, 29, **30**

F
fish, escovitch, 29, **30**
foo-foo, 24, **27**

fritters, banana, 39, **41**

G
garlic, 15
ginger, 15
beer, **42**, 43
ginger root, 15
grate, 14
grater, 13

I
ice, coconut, **38**, 39
ingredients, special, 14-15

J
Jamaica
akkra, 24, **26**
curried lamb, **34**, 35
duckunoo, 39, **40-41**
escovitch fish, 29, **30**
Jamaican beef patties, **32-33**
johnny cakes, 24, **26-27**
pepperpot soup, **18**, 20
rice and peas, 24, **25**
stamp and go, **28**, 29
Jamaican beef patties, **32-33**
johnny cakes, 24, **26-27**
jug jug, **36-37**

K
kale, 15

L
lamb, curried, **34**, 35
lard, 15

M
main dishes, 28
Betty's browned-down chicken,
4, **31**
Caribbean-style rice, 35, **36**
curried lamb, **34**, 35
escovitch fish, 29, **30**
Jamaican beef patties, **32-33**
jug jug, **36-37**
stamp and go, **28**, 29

menu, Caribbean, 16-17
metric conversion chart, 45
monosodium glutamate, 15

N
nutmeg, 15

O
okra, 15
cornmeal coo-coo, **23**, 24
oregano, 15

P
paprika, 15
peanut punch, **43**
peas, rice and, 24, **25**
peppercorns, 15
pepperpot
soup, **18**, 20
stew, 20, **21**
plantains, 15
foo-foo, 24, **27**
pone, sweet potato, 39, **40**
pork
pepperpot soup, **18**, 20
pepperpot stew, 20, **21**
Puerto Rico
asopao, 2, **22**
punch, peanut, **43**

R
rice
Caribbean-style, 35, **36**
and peas, 24, **25**
rolling pin, 13

S
sauté, 14
scald, 14
seafood
callaloo, **19**, 20
escovitch fish, 29, **30**
stamp and go, **28**, 29
seed, 14
side dishes, 23

akkra, 24, **26**
cornmeal coo-coo, **23,** 24
foo-foo, 24, **27**
johnny cakes, 24, **26-27**
rice and peas, 24, **25**
sieve, 13
sift, 14
simmer, 14
slotted spoon, 13
soup(s), 18
callaloo, **19,** 20
pepperpot, **18,** 20
special ingredients, 14-15
stamp and go, **28,** 29
stew(s), 18
asopao, 2, **22**
pepperpot, 20, **21**
suet, 15
sweet potato pone, 39, **40**

T
terms, cooking, 14
thyme, 15
tongs, 13
Trinidad and Tobago
Betty's browned-down chicken,
4, **31**
ginger beer, **42,** 43
peanut punch, **43**
rice and peas, 24, **25**

U
utensils, cooking, 13

Y
yeast, 15

ABOUT THE AUTHOR

Cheryl Davidson Kaufman was born and raised in Kingston, Jamaica. After attending college in Indiana, she moved to Minnesota on a whim and has lived there ever since. Kaufman spends most of her time managing a hospital cafeteria and playing keyboards with several reggae bands.

Kaufman was taught to cook by her grandmother, mother, and aunts, a group she considers to be "some of the best from-scratch cooks in the Caribbean," and she has always enjoyed spending hours in the kitchen. She particularly likes to cook for large groups—40 people is nothing—and loves to experiment with blending Midwestern and Caribbean cooking.

easy menu *ethnic* cookbooks

Cooking the **AFRICAN** Way
Cooking the **AUSTRALIAN** Way
Cooking the **AUSTRIAN** Way
Cooking the **CARIBBEAN** Way
Cooking the **CHINESE** Way
Cooking the **ENGLISH** Way
Cooking the **FRENCH** Way
Cooking the **GERMAN** Way
Cooking the **GREEK** Way
Cooking the **HUNGARIAN** Way
Cooking the **INDIAN** Way
Cooking the **ISRAELI** Way
Cooking the **ITALIAN** Way
Cooking the **JAPANESE** Way
Cooking the **KOREAN** Way
Cooking the **LEBANESE** Way
Cooking the **MEXICAN** Way
Cooking the **NORWEGIAN** Way
Cooking the **POLISH** Way
Cooking the **RUSSIAN** Way
Cooking the **SOUTH AMERICAN** Way
Cooking the **SPANISH** Way
Cooking the **THAI** Way
Cooking the **VIETNAMESE** Way
DESSERTS Around the World
HOLIDAY Cooking Around the World
VEGETARIAN Cooking Around the World